ROARSOME DINOSAURS 2022

This annual belongs to the

TOTALLY ROARSOME

....

ROAR!

DINOSAUR FACTS

The world of dinosaurs is **ROARSOME.** Start your prehistoric journey through this exciting book with these dino-tastic facts.

Dinosaurs ruled the Earth for over 200 million years. Humans have only been on Earth for 200 thousand years.

The largest dinosaur weighed 70 tonnes, that's 10 times heavier than an elephant!

Someone who studies dinosaurs is called a **PALAEONTOLOGIST.**

Birds are descended from a group of dinosaurs known as theropods.

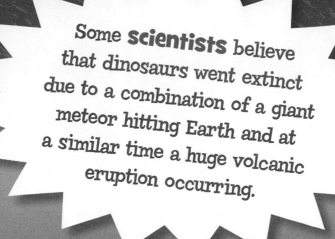

Some **scientists** believe that dinosaurs went extinct due to a combination of a giant meteor hitting Earth and at a similar time a huge volcanic eruption occurring.

At present, over 700 different types of dinosaurs have been identified. Palaeontologists believe there are many more new types yet to be discovered – how exciting!

The word 'dinosaur' comes from the Greek meaning of **TERRIBLE LIZARD.**

The smallest fully-grown dinosaur was only the size of a chicken.

Dinosaurs have been found on every continent around the world!

T REX!

Check out all these **ROARSOME** facts about the famous and ferocious T rex.

TYRANNOSAURUS REX

How do I say this?

tie-RAN-oh-sore-us

Diet: carnivorous (meat-eater)

When it lived: late Cretaceous, 68-66 million years ago

Found in: Canada, USA

Type: large theropod

Length: 12m

Weight: 7,000kg

DID YOU KNOW?

- T rex had 60 saw-edged and pointed teeth. Each tooth could be up to 20cm long, which is the size of a banana! Ouch!

ROAR!

- The T rex was one of the last dinosaurs from the Tyrannosaur family to evolve before the extinction of the dinosaurs.
- T rex had a big brain compared to other meat-eating dinosaurs. It also had an amazing sense of smell.

- T rex walked on two legs and balanced itself on them as birds do.
- T rex bite marks that have been found on Triceratops fossils show that the T rex could crunch through bone.
- It is believed that the T rex could run at about 20 miles per hour!
- T rex's little arms were too short to reach its mouth.
- It had a lifespan of about 30 years.

Tyrannosaurus rex means...
'TYRANT LIZARD KING'.

T REX JOKES

Is there anything better than a good joke? Well, yes – lots of ROARSOME, rib-tickling T rex jokes!

What do you get if you cross a T rex with explosives?
Dino-mite.

Where does a Tyrannosaurus rex sit when he comes to stay?
Anywhere he wants.

What do you call a T rex who hates to lose?
A saur loser.

What do you call a dinosaur's one-eyed dog?
A Do-you-think-he-saurus rex.

What do you call an anxious dinosaur?
A nervous rex.

MAMA!

What do you call a dinosaur car accident?
A Tyrannosaurus wreck.

What do you call a baby dinosaur?
A Wee rex.

What do you call a dinosaur after they break up with their girlfriend?
Tyrannosaurus ex.

What should you do if you see a T rex?
Hope that it doesn't see you!

Why did the Tyrannosaurus rex cross the road?
Because chickens hadn't evolved yet.

What do you call a group of dinosaurs who can sing?
A Tyranno-chorus.

How do you know if there is a dinosaur in your fridge?
The door won't shut.

ROAR!
with laughter!

What do you call a dinosaur who is a noisy sleeper?
A Tyranno-snore-us.

How do you ask a Tyrannosaur out for dinner?
"Tea, rex?"

9

VELOCIRAPTOR!

The fierce, feathery raptors were small but deadly dangerous!

VELOCIRAPTOR
How do I say this?
vel-OSS-ee-rap-tor

ROAR!

Velociraptor means
'QUICK PLUNDERER'

Diet: carnivorous (meat-eater)
When it lived: late Cretaceous, 74–70 million years ago
Found in: Mongolia
Type: small theropod
Length: 1.8m
Weight: 7kg

DID YOU KNOW?

- Velociraptors were covered in feathers.
- **Raptors likely hunted their prey solo, perhaps using their claws to clutch their prey rather than slash it.**
- The raptors in the film *Jurassic Park* were based on a Velociraptor relative, the Deinonychus antirrhopus, which was a much larger dinosaur that inhabited North America.
- Velociraptors ran on 2 legs.
- It is believed that the Velociraptor could run at about 24 miles per hour!
- **Palaeontologists believe that Velociraptors were nocturnal, which means they were awake during the night and slept during the day.**

- Some experts believe that Velociraptors' arms actually had feathers on them, as if they were small wings. They couldn't use these to fly though!
- **Velociraptors had an amazing sense of smell, which they used to efficiently hunt and track their prey.**

Yikes!

LET'S DOODLE!

This Velociraptor is missing its feathers! Can you draw them on its body?

Did you know?
As Velociraptors hunted at night, they would have had amazing eyesight.

Did you know?
It is believed Velociraptors had feathers to keep them warm or perhaps to 'talk' to others by waving their wings and tails.

The Velociraptor had a fearsome claw on each foot. Draw in the claws.

12

KEEP AN EYE ON THE SHADOWS

You never know what is lurking in the shadows in the prehistoric forests. Each box has one shadow that is different from the others, can you spot each different shadow?

Answers on pages 46-47

TRICERATOPS

Read on to learn all about everyone's favourite three-horned dinosaur.

TRICERATOPS
How do I say this?
tri-SERRA-tops

ROAR!

Diet: herbivore (plant-eater)
When it lived: late Cretaceous, 66-68 million years ago
Found in: USA
Type: ceratopsian
Length: 9m
Weight: 5,500kg

DID YOU KNOW?

- Triceratops moved around on all of its legs.
- Triceratops had a 'parrot-like' beak.

Triceratops means 'THREE HORNED FACE'

- Triceratops may have had as many as 800 teeth – imagine having to brush all of those!
- The frill on the back of the head could be nearly 1 metre across.
- The frill is thought to have protected the Triceratops' neck. Fossils have been found with teeth marks in them!

- The frill may also have been used as a way for different Triceratops to recognise each other.
- Triceratops is known for having three horns, but technically it only had two. The third smaller horn on the end of its nose is not made of bone, but from keratin – the same material that your nails and hair are made from.
- Unlike other horned dinosaurs, it is believed that Triceratops didn't live in groups called herds, but actually spent most of their lives alone.
- The Triceratops' skull was over one third of its entire body length.
- Its skull is one of the largest skulls ever recorded for a land animal.

15

LET'S DOODLE

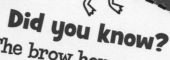

Triceratops had three horns on its head. Can you draw in the horns onto the Triceratops below?

Did you know?
The brow horns could each grow to a metre in length!

Can you draw a pattern on the bony frill?

WHERE'S MY MUMMY?

How many leaves does the Triceratops pass on the route?

Uh oh, this little Triceratops has been separated from its mummy. Can you discover which path will lead the baby back to safety?

1 2 3 4 5

STEGOSAURUS

This slow-moving herbivore is best known for its armour plates on its back. Let's learn about the Stegosaurus.

STEGOSAURUS
How do I say this?
STEG-oh-SORE-us

Stegosaurus means
'ROOF LIZARD'

Diet: herbivore (plant-eater)
When it lived: late Jurassic, 155-145 million years ago
Found in: USA
Type: armoured dinosaur
Length: 9m
Weight: 3,100kg

DID YOU KNOW?

- Stegosaurus was about the size of a bus.
- **Stegosaurus would have defended itself from predators with its powerful spiked tail.**

- The spikes on the tail are known as thagomizers.
- The Stegosaurus had 17 plates across its back. They were not attached to its skeleton.
- It is not known what exactly the plates were used for – perhaps they were for protection, a way for different Stegosauruses to recognise each other or perhaps to regulate their body temperature.

- Compared with the size of its body, a Stegosaurus had a small head and brain.
- **The Stegosaurus's brain was the size and shape of a bent hotdog.**
- It is thought that Stegosauruses travelled in big family groups, or herds.
- Its front legs were much shorter than its back legs.
- **Stegosaurus and its relatives are closely related to the Ankylosaurus.**

ROAR!

LET'S DOODLE

A Stegosaurus had a series of bony plates along its back. Can you draw in the missing plates?

Did you know?
A Stegosaurus fed on plants close to the ground.

Did you know?
Palaeontologists aren't sure about the function of the plates. They might have been used for defence or to keep the Stegosaurus cool.

Can you doodle a cool pattern onto the Stegosaurus' skin?

ADD SOME COLOUR TOO!

WORDSEARCH

Can you find all these words hidden in the grid below?
Look forwards, downwards and diagonally.

```
N D C A V T B O N Y P L A T E S
H Z H E Y H C R E J K B O C T Y
E R O O F L I Z A R D O R H S I
R S T R C U P F X I A N K E T C
B I R U J S W Y G H N S I E S J
I T A O G I A L F J U P R K L U
V A L L A D U B X R M I P D I R
O R P R O H R Y U S H K D T A A
R X S H X S D A S Y E E P R N S
E P L A N T S R A R X D L A N S
N U I X O O U M G B Q T S O U I
D S T Z G I S O E M U A H R P C
A I A E A L Y U J J W I E Z A L
T D T C C M R R X K N L R H T O
E S K Z O J U F T C V P I X S W
```

- [ ] STEGOSAURUS
- [ ] HERBIVORE
- [ ] BONY PLATES
- [ ] BRAIN
- [ ] PLANTS
- [ ] CHEEK
- [ ] JURASSIC
- [ ] ROOF LIZARD
- [ ] SPIKED TAIL
- [ ] ARMOUR

DIPLODOCUS

ROAR!

The Diplodocus was the longest dinosaur that ever lived, let's learn all about it.

DIPLODOCUS
How do I say this?
DIP-low DOCK-us

Diet: herbivore (plant-eater)
When it lived: late Jurassic, 155-145 million years ago
Found in: USA
Type: sauropod
Length: 26m
Weight: 2,000kg

DID YOU KNOW?

- Most of the Diplodocus' length was taken up by its neck and tail.
- Diplodocus probably held its long neck level to the ground. It wouldn't have been able to hold its head much higher than its body.
- The Diplodocus' front legs were shorter than its back legs.
- Diplodocus had five toes on each of its large feet.
- Its back legs were very powerful, and it is thought that it could rear up on its back legs to reach leaves higher up on trees.
- The Diplodocus' body was balanced by its long, heavy tail. The tail could have been used as a weapon against attackers.
- Diplodocus' nose was high up on its forehead and not on the end of its snout!
- The spine of the Diplodocus, including the neck and tail, had almost 100 vertebrae (the bones that make up the spine).
- It had a very small head compared to the size of its body and would have had a very small brain.
- A Diplodocus had rows of teeth, a bit like a comb.

Diplodocus means **'DOUBLE BEAM'**

OUT OF LINE!

Circle the correct answer in each line.

Diplodocuses are known for having long necks and long tails. Can you find the correct dinosaur in each line?

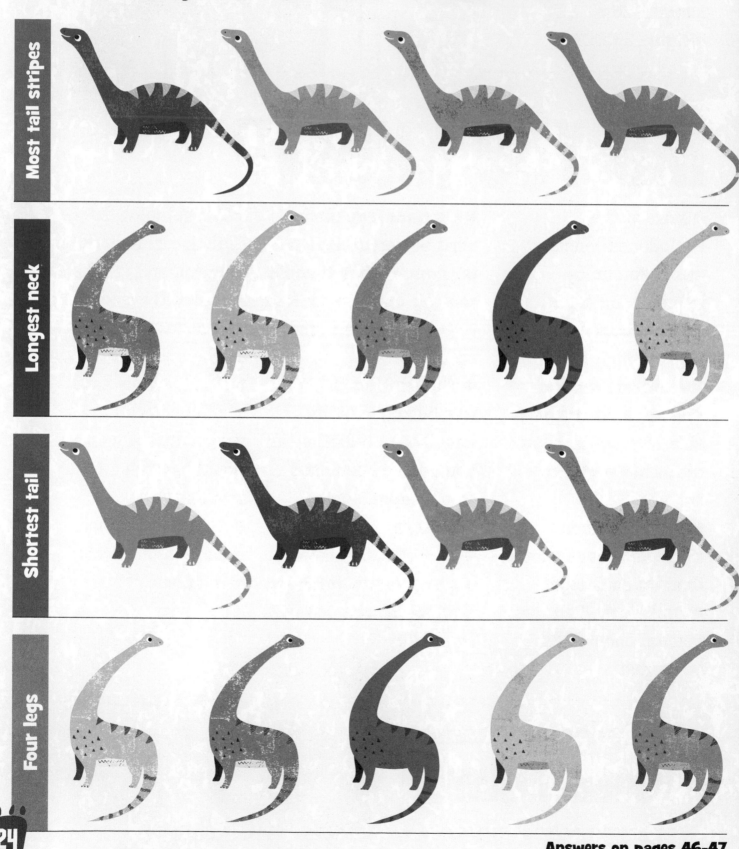

Most tail stripes

Longest neck

Shortest tail

Four legs

24

SPOT THE DIFFERENCE

Look closely at these prehistoric scenes. Can you spot 10 differences between the pictures?

Colour in a bone each time you find a difference.

ANKYLOSAURUS

An Ankylosaurus was one of the largest armoured dinosaurs ever to roam Earth.

ANKYLOSAURUS
How do I say this?
An-KIE-loh-sore-us

Diet: herbivore (plant-eater)
When it lived: late Cretaceous, 74-67 million years ago
Found in: Canada, USA
Type: armoured dinosaur
Length: 7m
Weight: 4,000kg

ROAR!

DID YOU KNOW?

- An Ankylosaurus was one of the largest armoured dinosaurs.
- **The Ankylosaurus had a wide, heavily armoured skull and a large tail club.**
- It had a large stomach for digesting plant material.
- The top of the Ankylosaurus was almost completely covered with thick armour, much like the skin of a crocodile.
- It had two rows of spikes along its body.
- **An Ankylosaurus' body was wider than it was deep, so they were very difficult to attack.**
- The only part of the Ankylosaurus' body that wasn't covered in armour was its underbelly.
- A predator would have to flip an Ankylosaurus over first; it is believed the armour and spikes were strong enough to break their teeth!
- The club at the end of the tail was made from vertebrae (bones in the spine) that were fused together.
- Even the Ankylosaurus' eyelids were armoured!
- **Its nostrils were on the side of its head.**
- The top speed of an Ankylosaurus is estimated to only have been up to six miles per hour.

LET'S DOODLE

Did you know?
There haven't been enough fossils of the Ankylosaurus' feet to determine if they had toes – although it is believed they had five toes.

An Ankylosaurus was covered in bony armour and spikes to protect it from predators. Can you cover this Ankylosaurus with armour and spikes?

Ankylosaurus had a huge clubbed tail. Can you draw the clubbed tail in?

MUNCH TIME

Ankylosaurus was huge, but it was a herbivore and only ate plants! Can you find the one leaf on the page which the Ankylosaurus wants to eat?

The leaf is not blue.

The leaf is not on a tree.

The leaf does not have stripes.

The leaf only has 5 points.

The leaf has spots.

The leaf is orange.

Answers on pages 46–47

SPINOSAURUS

A Spinosaurus is known for the large sail on its back, it was thought to be the longest meat-eater to roam Earth.

ROAR!

Diet: carnivore (meat-eater)
When it lived: late Cretaceous, 95-70 million years ago
Found in: Egypt, Morocco
Type: large theropod
Length: 18m
Weight: 4,000kg

SPINOSAURUS
How do I say this?
SPINE-oh-SORE-us

DID YOU KNOW?

- A Spinosaurus could grow up to 18m, which makes it the longest meat-eater. It was longer and heavier than a T rex!
- The Spinosaurus is only known from incomplete fossils.
- Most of the best fossil remains were destroyed during bombing raids during World War II.
- **It is believed that they lived both on land and in the water, much like a crocodile.**
- A Spinosaurus had a long, narrow skull. Its eyes and nostrils were at the top and towards the end of the snout, again like a crocodile. This would have allowed it to breathe even with most of its snout underwater.
- **Its teeth were straight and conical shaped.**
- It is believed that a Spinosaurus mainly ate fish.
- The sail on the Spinosaurus' spine was probably used for social displays or so different animals could recognise each other.
- The spine sail was as high as two metres and when a Spinosaurus arched its back, the sail would rise up.

Spinosaurus means...
'THORN LIZARD'

LETS'S DOODLE

Did you know? It is believed the spine sail was used to communicate with other Spinosaurus.

Spinosaurus is known for the huge spiny sail spine on its back. Can you complete the spine sail on Spinosaurus?

Doodle a pattern on the spine sail.

32

JIGSAW JUMBLE

Can you find the right pieces to fill the gaps
and complete the picture?

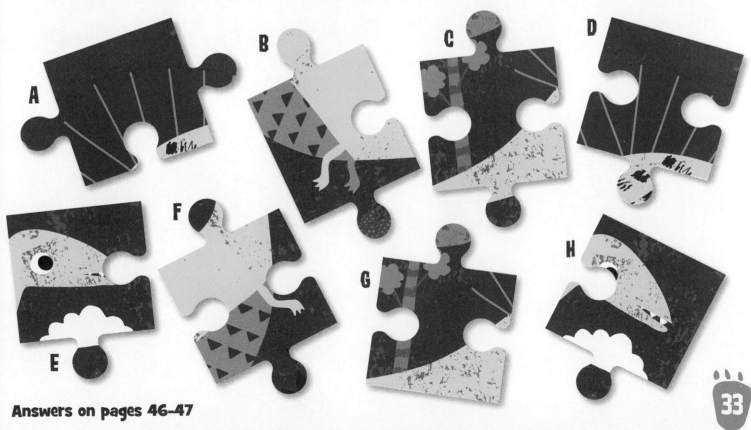

PTEROSAUR

Flying reptiles called Pterosaurs dominated the skies at the same time that dinosaurs roamed Earth.

Pterosaur means...
'WINGED LIZARD'

PTEROSAUR
How do I say this?
TEH-ruh-saw

Diet: carnivore (meat-eater)
When it lived: late Triassic, around 215 million years ago
Found in: worldwide

DID YOU KNOW?

- Pterosaurs and dinosaurs evolved separately from a common ancestor that lived 230 million years ago.
- More than 150 different species of Pterosaurs have been identified.
- The smallest Pterosaur, Nemicolopterus, had a wingspan of just 25cm.
- The Pterosaur Quetzalcoatlus was the largest creature ever to fly. It had a wingspan of 10 metres which is larger than many two-seater airplanes!
- They were the first vertebrates (animals with a spine) to fly.
- Paleontologists believe that Pterosaurs were actually fluffy! This means that they were probably warm-blooded like bats and birds.
- Recently discovered fossil tracks suggest that Pterosaurs walked on all-fours, folding up their wings like umbrellas.
- By the time a Pterosaur hatched, its wings were fully formed. It probably could have taken off shortly after it hatched.
- Pterosaur bones were hollow.
- Pterosaurs' closest living relatives are crocodiles and birds.
- It is believed that some Pterosaurs could reach speeds of up to 75mph when flying.

LETS'S DOODLE

Add some big wings to this Pterosaur to help him fly high in the sky.

Can you fill the rest of the sky with Pterosaurs?

HOW MANY?

How many winged wonders can you spot on this page? Fill in the answers below.

1 How many Pterosaurs can you count in total? ....

2 How many green ones are there? ....

3 How many blue ones are there? ....

4 Are there more pink Pterosaurs or red ones? ....

Answers on pages 46-47

DINOSAUR EGGS

Check out these 10 cracking facts about dinosaur eggs.

1 **Dinosaurs reproduced** by laying eggs, much like modern-day reptiles and birds.

2 As a general rule, eggs laid by meat-eating dinosaurs (theropods) were longer than they were wide, while the eggs of most other dinosaurs (bird-like, plant-eaters) laid more spherical eggs.

3 **Many dinosaur eggs** never got the chance to hatch as predators would gobble them up before they could hatch.

4 **Dinosaur eggs** would have been laid by female dinosaurs and contained a developing dinosaur embryo.

5 Dinosaur eggs are more symmetrical than bird eggs.

6 **Some dinosaurs** laid eggs in a spiral shape in a nest they dug out and covered with vegetation to keep it warm.

7
Baby dinosaurs grew very quickly after hatching; in six weeks they might double in size.

8
No matter what the full-size adult of the dinosaur ended up being, no eggs have been found larger than half a metre in diameter.

9
Dinosaur eggs varied in shape, size, colour and texture. Some have been found to be greenish in colour.

10
It is believed that female dinosaurs laid multiple eggs at the same time, perhaps between 3 and 20 eggs per batch.

WORDSEARCH

Can you find all these words hidden in the grid below?
Look forwards, downwards and diagonally.

```
B N B O N E S E S D N S A U Q O
T E N R F G H P C H X T W H A R
H E T O Z G E R K S O F O D D H
D R B Z C S R O O G X R L E H L
N O E P T S B V R Y X G N O E O
F A O C A R N I V O R E B T R N
R S V Y E L D A E K X L K W B V
I R C A Y X H J A D X C W S I A
L O E N D G T T K E X L R K V I
L M E L H T E I Y R X A C G O R
E E T I S H E A N O X W M L R F
I X U O B A T P I C X S X A E H
A S X N K J H N A K T Z T S L S
M N P T A V X U E J X R H S P Q
S F O S S I L C F L U T C E C A
```

EXTINCT FOSSIL HERBIVORE ROCK

FRILL HORNS CLAWS EGGS

TEETH CARNIVORE BONES

40 Answers on pages 46–47

LETS'S COLOUR

Colour in the dinosaurs relaxing in this swamp.

DINOSAUR FOSSILS

Everything we know about dinosaurs, we learn from finding fossils. Learn 10 great facts about fossils on these pages.

1 The word 'fossil' comes from a Latin word (fossus) meaning 'having been dug up'.

2 **Palaeontologists** are like detectives who examine the evidence that extinct animals left behind

3 **Fossils can look like bone**, but they aren't! Fossils are made from rock which is shaped exactly as the object that was originally there.

4 Dinosaur fossils have been found all over the world.

5 HOW FOSSILS ARE MADE...

• The object will be buried.
• This gets squashed and turned into rock.
• Water then goes into the bones which turns them into rock by leaving behind minerals where the bones once were.

6

Fossils are incredibly rare! This is because when an animal dies, everything (including the bones) decompose very quickly so there is nothing left to fossilise. It is only when they are buried quickly that fossilisation works.

7

Finding a whole dinosaur bone, let alone a whole skeleton is incredibly rare.

8 Bones aren't the only things that Palaeontologists find in the ground and rocks, they can also find footprint tracks, skin and feather impressions and coprolites (dinosaur poo!).

9 Fossilised bones are very fragile and often break while they are being dug out of the ground. Palaeontologists protect the bones to transport them by covering them in plaster of Paris – similar to how doctors put a case on broken bones.

10

In some cases, rock and fossil bone look very similar. One simple and quick way to tell the difference is to lick it – if it sticks to your tongue, it is a fossil and if it doesn't, it is rock.

DINOSAUR HUNTER

Can you find all the items listed in the panel in the picture below? Tick them off as you find them.

Answers on pages 46-47

Can you find...?

- 1 volcano
- 2 T rex
- 3 Diplodocuses
- 4 Velociraptors
- 5 Stegosauruses
- 6 dinosaur eggs

ANSWERS

PAGE 13

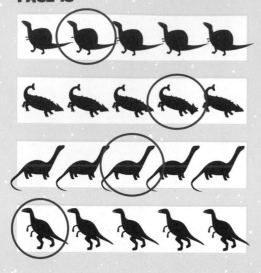

PAGE 21

N D C A V T (B O N Y P L A T E S)
H Z H E Y H (C R E J K B O C) T Y
(H E R) (R O O F L I Z A R D) O (R H E) S I
(R) S T R C U P F X I A N (K) E (K) T C
(B) I R U J S W Y G H N (S) I (E) S (J)
(I) T A O G I A L F J U P R (K) L U
(V) A L L A D U B X R M I P D T R
(O) R P R O H R Y U S H K D T A A
(R) X S H X S (D) A S Y E E P R N S
(E) (P L A N T S) R A R X D L A N S
N U I X C O U M G B Q T A I S O I
D S T Z G I S O E M U A H R Z C
A I A E A L Y U J J W I E Z A L
T D T C C M R J R X K N L R H T O
E (S K Z O J U F T C V P I X S W)

PAGE 24

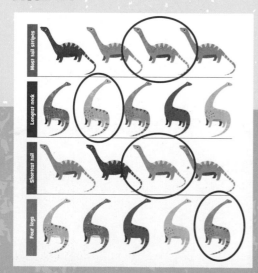

PAGE 17

Route 3. He passes
5 leaves on the way

PAGE 25